She Was All Her Crazy

She Was All Her Crazy

A collection of poetry by

Tiffany Ann Whitten

Self-published by Tiffany Ann Whitten

ISBN: 978-0-359-11247-0

First U.S. edition 2018

This book is dedicated to:

Sheri (My mother and friend):
Who always believed that I could
build a rocket to the moon if I wanted to.
Without you, I would be completely lost.
Thank you, for everything.

Tracy (My ride or die):
Who continues to be my conscience
and who allows me to sing my heart out on long
car rides when my world is crumbling or exciting
(though my singing is terrible)!
My life would be utterly incomplete without
you in it.

Love and Hugs,
~T

She Was All Her Crazy

She was all her crazy,
owned it with a passionate fury,
the madness settling in
(fitting in)
quite nicely like a glove fitted just for her.
She wore it so well – the distain, the heartbreak
the never-ending criticism of others as they passed her by,
reading them like an open book
(her favorite book)
that she's read a million times before.
The darkness in her eyes tells the story of her life,
ask her and she'll only tell you- "I've been through a few things."
Never letting you into the place where she hides
all of her fears, all of her sorrows, all of her pain.
Perpetuating negativity seeps from her pores,
finding fault in everything, even herself –
mostly herself.
Drifting along this life with a chip resting oh-so
comfortably upon her shoulder,
her failings lying just beneath her skin,
quietly waiting for the disappointments to make their
cunning appearance, she braces herself for the
carnage while shielding her wounded heart.
She embraces her bitterness with her open arms,
accepting that she sees the human form as a revolting
carcass tempted by the shiny things, but not her,
never her.
She honors her crazy like a fashion piece,
displaying it proudly as it drapes around her neck,
always holding the world at arm's length.

But on Paper

I write because at times I'm socially awkward,
this illusion that the thoughts form into graceful words that escape my lips lives strong inside my mind.
Pen to paper I write my soul,
forming my emotions into words that sometimes make sense.
I let go of expectations that have been placed upon me,
freely allow the world to be shut off,
I accept the pain that might follow,
I embrace the hope that I dream about.
A window into my soul,
a glimpse into pieces of me that I have allowed to be scattered around,
for out loud I will not share my inner most emotions,
but on paper it all falls out.

Memories Dance

You see that I've crawled back into myself,
you ask me where I've gone too,
honestly,
I cannot share that with you
(I cannot speak it out loud)
for the places I go are often dark and damaging,
I need to figure my own way out.
Illusions of melancholy float about,
delicately defining who I am,
with no thought to the small hint of who I might be without it.
The wishing for everlasting happiness doesn't sit
well with me for very long,
my self-conscious takes over to push me back down,
the constant reminder telling me
"That you, my dear," won't ever be good enough for keeping.
I try to not listen,
hoping that it's all lies,
quiet memories dance seductively reminding
me of truths I dare not speak of
(and wishing to forget)
but in the dark I know,
my subconscious is right.

My Drug

I've never tried a drug before her.
I'm addicted to her smell, her touch, her taste –
her complete indecisiveness about me.
I keep crawling back,
knowing there will be pain mixed with pleasure.
I pull away abruptly at times,
trying to get a grasp on my emotions that want to be
wrapped up in her,
constantly aching for her,
but I find my way back,
like a moth to a flame,
knowing there's a chance of me burning.
The risk of permanent good-byes I can't accept,
this constant need for her sends my soul on fire,
a bliss that captures my attention,
I become fixated on everything beautiful about her,
which is – everything.
Velvet lips that possess poison to draw me into her,
unfold myself into her when her blue eyes scan my soul,
I melt inside myself so she can't see the level
of control she has over me,
my drug.

I Deserve Better

She damaged me in ways my heart can only bleed of,
her perpetual back and forth with me,
caused my anxiety to erupt and my insecurities to soar to the skies of infinite despair.
I'm a convenience to her,
her fake honey words reeled me in and spit me back out at her leisure,
leaving me each time more jaded,
my wounds more exposed for all to see.
She taught me well,
with her selfish demons floating in and out of my life like nothing else mattered in this world but her
(but oh! She was certainly wrong).
I picked myself up off the floor,
realized that she might have bent me for a short time-
bravo to her as I slow clap my hands for all that I see she is.
I am not broken, I am not unfixable,
I still have the ability to fly though my wings are tattered.
I finally see the truth of what we were,
a life lesson for me to grow into something more than I accepted within myself.
I say thank you now to her for teaching me that love doesn't look like enticing fingers in shadows only to push me away when I get near,
it's not consuming the spaces that hide within only to fill them with empty words that don't match actions,
it's not constant taking until the other is left slowly bleeding out on white carpet that stains.
Love is a fragile contact between two souls that should have mutual respect,
it should be cherished in ways that allow you to breathe when the world fills your lungs with hate.
I was able to find bandages to cover the cuts that she carved recklessly into my skin,
able to sew the deeper gashes that will certainly show scars,
but I am alive and I have learned – I deserve better.

Drown

I am lost in a place that has me pining away for you,
all the blinds are closed,
the doors are locked,
yet the draft creeps in with a bitter savage wind that rips
into my soul.
I wish to take the feelings of love and passion from my
vocabulary,
float them down the river or tie them to a balloon
that disappears into the dark galaxy.
Every feeling that I have never wanted to have is crashing
into me like a giant wave that leaves me gasping for air
(am I slowly downing?).
I fell for you at a rapid pace,
you fell alongside me,
yet every chance you get to push me away –
you take it,
as if you're taking the very last life vest to save only your damn self,
leaving me to find my own way,
to figure out how to not drown.

For Her

I sit quietly,
waiting for the vibration
of the phone that doesn't come.
Mostly so I can avoid it so not to appear hopelessly
desperate – because with her I'm holding my breath,
thinking of every thought of her,
willing every thought to be with her- secretly willing,
pleading her to be mine in a way that is lasting and endearing -
it won't last,
I know.
Her and I,
we are like stars that collide,
stars that explode and end up going into separate directions
then fading into the endless galaxy,
I wish to have hope for love,
hope for something that I can hold onto with hands
that cradle the softness of the bright stars.
I tell her – I tell her – it is what it is,
I tell her my heart isn't intertwined with hers,
I tell her that I don't care,
I tell her to do what she wants to do,
I tell her – I tell her shit that I think she wants to hear,
not to push her out,
not to push her away from me,
but to slightly scare her,
to not make her want to leave me,
to not make her want to forget about me.
In the dark,
I long for her in secrets that whisper alone
within this loneliness that envelopes me with a brokenness
that keeps me constantly aching for her.

Free to Fly

She doesn't apologize for the expected chaos
that is her life
(she's used to it).
Bravely she walks this world,
her head held high.
she's been through enough in this lifetime to see through the deceit
(you can't fool her).
You have no idea the pain she's endured,
the struggles she's overcome – she won't tell you,
but quietly you will understand that she's been through it all,
survived a hell that you cannot begin to grasp.
Too many times she's been held captive,
but now she's found her wings,
she will not be placed in a cage
(by you or anyone)
she needs to be free to fly –
to soar.

Missing You

I miss you in ways that are innocent,
when the sun is hovering above the sky and the birds carelessly sing,
I look over to see your face,
forgetting you're no longer standing with my hand in yours.
I breath in the morning dew when I first open my eyes,
remembering every detail about your face,
hearing your laugher inside my head,
smelling you when I walk by flowers that are just beginning to bloom.
I go on living,
or pretending to live,
all the while missing you in the simplest tasks that I do.
Your toothbrush still remains in the exact spot where you left it,
I can't force myself to throw it away,
my pillow smells of you and one day I will wash it,
but I'm just not ready today.
I wear your socks,
even when my feet are not cold,
a small item of yours that you left behind.
Your photograph on my nightstand,
I can't bring myself to rip it up,
so, it sits mocking me with your smile,
while your life goes on without me,
I live in a place that constantly reminds me of you.
One day maybe the missing will stop,
maybe I can live without your name always upon my lips,
maybe I can wish for someone else's skin,
maybe I can dream without dreaming of you,
but until then I live in a place where I am perpetually missing you.

The Wreckage

The wreckage from my past collides
(on occasion)
with my now.
Filling the voided holes with confusion,
allowing insecurities to linger just a little too long.
Scratching the surface,
I beg to be set free,
fearing that the damage cannot be undone.
Below the darkness I quiver in this shallow state,
haunting by illusions of failed attempts at living.
Behind my closed soul I attempt to scream,
my voice goes unheard,
only silence escapes me.
fingers dance a whimsical plea,
beckoning me to enter the carnage of my unsettled bygones,
closing my eyes and reply in a whispered tone,
that I'm going back to that decay.

Relevant

My breath escapes me when I see her,
somehow,
she saved me,
though she doesn't know it.
She broke into the sorrow of my soul,
pulled me from the wreckage that was my life.
I was simply existing in this world,
walking along a path that wasn't mine.
Broken and worn,
I lost my own voice and believed that dreaming
wasn't meant for me anymore.
She gave me hope and clarity,
told me to scream until I became relevant
because she believed that's what I am,
relevant.

The Blue One

She lost hope in the twilight hours while seeking refuge from herself.
She throws around the word crazy like it's candy to be passed out during a hospital stay
(she'll take the blue one).
Her past haunts her,
travels near and far to sabotage her efforts at living,
she's reminded of her failures when she looks in the mirror,
her anxieties unravel and wrap her up like a warm blanket.
She believes she deserves chaos and destruction,
constantly bathing in it,
then wonders why her world is so messy,
tattered with heartbreaking consequences.
Taking the blue pill if prescribed to her,
it is her favorite color after all.

Her Worth

Misguided by her jaded past she doesn't know her worth.
This beautiful soul with a fire inside that burns bright,
but she doesn't see it.
Always the pessimist,
shielding herself from falling,
from disappointment,
from heartbreak.
Expecting the collapse,
she embraces it
(it will eventually come – she knows it).
If only she could see herself through my eyes,
no time for bullshit,
she's as real as they come,
telling you honest words even when it hurts.
Her smile goes on for miles and lights up night skies,
(she doesn't know it).
Brilliant mind with a forgiving heart,
she has the ability to make you believe you can do anything,
be anything.
Her biggest fan is me,
I see her raw beauty and her soft soul,
despite wanting to be in the shadows (undisturbed).
I wish she knew that her worth is so much more
then she believes it to be.

Empty Life

I can't continue to give my heart away for false hopes and empty promises because the reality of it is- there's not much left for me to give away.
Most of my heart has turned into dust particles,
Blown away into the night skies- all but forgotten.
I long to remember what believing in happily ever after even felt like,
to try to hold it in my hand,
to have hope of unconditional love,
unfortunately the dream has faded,
leaving lies that shattered like glass.
I long for a breath of fresh air,
for the sun's rays to touch my skin,
for a tomorrow that doesn't look like an empty life.

Coffee

We sip coffee while holding pleasant conversations.
My soul concentrates on her eyes,
desperately attempting to locate the emotions she keeps quiet
within.
I see it,
somewhere hidden inside,
she finds me a bit chaotic at times,
she loves me too much to say aloud I'm eccentric,
a relief I sense washing over her that today,
I'm on my best behavior.
I dread getting so lost somewhere within my darkness
that I am unable to find my way back,
yet,
here I am looking at her and I realize,
she should be my home,
the beacon to pull me back when the madness stirs,
when the world becomes bleak and hopeless,
why isn't she?

Our Demise

The should haves and the what ifs float around like balloons ready to be popped.
Our demise began the day that we met,
slowly encouraging one another to fail with quiet encouraging words.
We were not meant for always,
our days started the count down and we often wonder how we even made it as long as we did.
I place blame on you for you lying,
taking my own blame for not compromising more.
We got stuck in this rut of daily lives
that we forgot how to actually be alive.
Our demise was an explosion waiting to happen,
the course of our lives floated down a river of bitter sorrows,
life lesson learned is that some things are not everlasting,
and sometimes good-bye is better than living in unhappy.
We both pause to look back at memories that unfolded,
nothing everything was bad,
remember the good and place the bad on the shelf,
be hopeful in a tomorrow that is filled with cordial light and forgiving hopes.

Not Ready

I wrote a letter for you,
detailing my faults,
outlining my shortcomings,
but I burned it.
I don’t want you to see the damage that lies within
(though you probably already do).
I fear one day you’ll wake up and see me,
see me for who I really am,
an unsophisticated loner with a talent for destruction.
At first glance I’m a shell of poise and confidence,
but dig a little deeper I lack promise to be anything but
Self-doubting and selfish,
a chilling representation of who I really am at the core.
This mask I don on tightly
(ensuring all fastens are secure)
helps me forget my past,
forget my sorrows.
I wish to take it off and be free,
but then you will see me,
really see me,
and I’m not ready just yet.

I Fall

I fall in and outside of myself,
reeling sideways and behind,
turning over and under,
trying to identify my thoughts,
but they rapidly slip and fall into the night sky,
like a blanket made from only words.
Reaching and tugging,
I scream to catch my breath,
to find a place of belonging,
yet I fall further below,
further within this hollow world,
this place where I can't find any light.
Illusions of life flashing and morphing,
I just let go and give in,
thinking that it's not giving up,
it's just pondering the what's and the if's,
you know,
the trappings of life,
misguided failings and half-truths reviled,
secret torments served on a silver platter for me to feast upon
(and I do)
to save myself,
to save my soul,
I just fall.

Fantasies

She keeps me up at night,
my thoughts stirring relentlessly in the dark.
I wonder how soft her skin would feel on my lips
and her body pressed against mine.
Infatuation when she smiles my direction,
my stomach flutters until I force myself to look away
(but I don't want to).
Does she know she's beautiful?
I imagine her tongue wrapped with mine,
her fingers caressing my back causing me to ache,
and I stand in awe.
One look has me daydreaming thoughts of her,
wanting to be wrapped up in a blanket with her,
wanting to feel my hands in her hair,
wanting to - get lost in her.
Open my eyes now back to reality that she might be too far away,
too out of my league,
but I'll always have my fantasies when she comes back to me.

Wrong Time

I dared to dream in colors that were as vivacious as the sun
radiating in the bluest sky,
even though I knew better.
Each glimpse of happiness I captured,
I tried to contain the memories in a jar,
but they float away when I open the lid to peek inside,
trying to recall the moments of you and I.
Bittersweet realization that soulmates exist,
but they can be fleeting,
still I tried to hold onto something tangible for as long as I could,
pretending my emotions were not reckless,
lying to myself that I could ignore my sweaty palms
and racing heartbeat when you smiled
(I fell).
Letting you go has been a torment for me,
perfect person,
wrong time.

But I Won't

This life is full of uncertainty,
I wander
(losing myself)
in the bitterness of tragic souls.
Hidden in the shadows of a life of discontent for an ordinary way.
Beckon me to run wild with rage,
fill my heart with black ashes of yesterday's sorrows – but I won't.
For today I am free and my soul soars somewhere in the light
(too far for my body to see).

Wolf Covered in Sheep's Skin

I wanted a safe place to lay my head,
instead I sat upon a bed of thorns mixed with nails.
Wondering how I got here,
hoping my final destination wasn't this damp place filled with the grim reality that you've become my worst waking nightmare.
In the loneliness I walk beside the shadows,
realizing that I held hands with the wolf covered in sheep's skin.
You were a valuable life lesson to learn,
lies seeping from your pores,
I hope you're happy in the destruction that you've created,
basking in your bullshit,
someone else will believe your fake truths.
As for me,
I found myself in the rubble,
disoriented from the light since I bathed in the darkness for too long,
but I found the light that you hid from me.

Called Living

I was drowning in my circumstances,
deeding my soul on empty promises,
lacking the ability to know any other life
(until)
You found me in this lonesome place,
opened my eyes to the unhappiness inside my beating heart.
I understood,
without words that I was better,
deserved better,
than this decomposing selfless void that I was
calling a life.

Remind Me

I pull away from her,
the daylight surfaces hazily against the night sky,
my demons won't allow me to stay,
for I've been vulnerable for her before,
cut myself open for her before,
handed my heart over to her before,
she left me to rot,
like a carcass that was chewed and spit out on the roadside,
wishing for vultures that never came to finish me off.
I'm certain this will be my last time,
blocking her from my brain,
even her sad eyes search mine as she speaks to me in a hushed whispered tone,
telling me that she feels she no longer exists in my life.
I let her walk away and close the door before she can look back to see me sighing a breath of relief,
hoping I can be strong when my heart wants to be so fucking weak (for her – only for her).
Remind me again that she's bad for my soul,
because when she reaches out for me I can't help but to extend my hand,
looking down she grabs me,
only to turn me into her yoyo.
Remind me to not answer my phone when her face fills my screen
because I am too weak to let the voicemail pick up,
every time she calls I'm quick to pick up,
when she texts I'm too eager to reply,
knowing- knowing full well she will pull me in with captivating eyes,
with love that devours me like I've never seen the sun,
this constant ache for her that never fills,
because as soon as she has me wrapped up around her finger,
she discards me with waving good-bye fingertips,
leaving my soul crushed for what was once mine
(but it really wasn't ever mine).
Remind me again that I am better off not knowing her kind of love,
because in the dark I crave her,
even though I know she only wants me when she's lonely.

Drown Myself in You

I want to be ravaged,
taken to a place of ecstasy where my head leaves my body.
Breathing in seduction,
letting the empty parts of my soul fill with passion and desire.
Losing myself somewhere between the now and the then,
my thoughts cannot focus and life slowly melts away into the darkness.
Allow me to let go and drown myself in you
(escaping the world within your fingertips).

Still Haunt

Beneath the surface of unsettled past I linger.
Fighting to forget dark memories that still haunt,
turn on the lights,
someone,
anyone.

Seeking Your Forgiveness

I wish to tell you so many things,
but writing is always easier for me.
Perhaps it's the way I can write honestly,
without having to look anyone in the eyes,
or the fact that I can erase anything that is displeasing or bullshit.
I sat today thinking of you,
thinking of us,
my faults magnified and I couldn't look away.
I was forced to see my life objectively and I thought…
I'm quite selfish.
I found myself saddened by the path I have chosen,
this path where I am above everything.
Cringing at the person I have become
(or maybe I've always been).
Seeking your forgiveness,
to love me despite my many faults and idiosyncrasies.
I vow to try to show you what my heart already knows,
which is because of you I'm a better person,
despite the lack of me telling or showing you.

She Wants

She wants to be loved for the crazy that she is,
someone who caresses her anger issues with a kind hand,
someone who allows her to be selfish without questioning,
someone who accepts that she is a weathered brutal storm.
Good days come few and far between,
too often her journey leads her to self-loathing and bitterness,
often hiding under the covers because she is at war with the universe.
She makes strides to fix the damage she's broke,
more times than not- set-backs make her question her existence,
she will take it out on you,
for you should be different, better, nothing.
Her anger will lash out at you
(be prepared)
for when she's in her manic rage you are the enemy.
She will eventually fall into a sadness which she cannot escape,
this too- is your fault.
Nothing you will ever do will be good enough for her,
mostly because she doesn't feel good enough for herself.
Take the lies and the cheating if you're able to,
for she wants you to accept her at her absolute worst,
she wants you to be her puppet on a string,
she wants you to understand that she believes she's too broken for fixing.

From Below

From below the emptiness resurfaces,
boiling over onto my current happiness,
seeking to poison the life I've created.
From below the self-loathing stirs,
bringing in a hopelessness that I can't escape or ignore.
From below the heartache rears its ugliness,
capturing my soul into a vice that stings in places that I cannot
begin to even speak of.
From below I fight to claw back to the top,
to feel some kind of sunlight upon my skin.
The depths of my inner injustice pulling me down,
wreaking havoc that no one else can see.

I Will Try

Sitting in this dark abyss,
crowded by faces unknown,
I deserve more from this life than what?
Struggling deep down to survive,
a hopeless disaster born with a plastic spoon,
denying that I am anything but complicated,
miserable and decaying.
Although,
you're my single reason I hold onto this belief that I am
honorable,
lovable,
anything but ordinary.
This life with you,
my peaceful everything,
embodies all that is good in this world.
For you see me at my worst,
my failings,
my misery,
yet you stay.
Forever pushing me to think I'm worth the bluest skies and the
darkness isn't meant for me.
This tangible happy existence,
I can stretch my fingers and almost reach.
I don't understand how you see my wretched heart
and believe it can turn into a butterfly,
but for you,
my sweet dream,
I will try.

All That I See

When the rest of the world was asleep
her soft voice broke up with me over the telephone.
I hung onto the line with both of us weeping,
knowing that when I pushed end - our lives would be disconnected,
I wasn't ready.
The darkness crept in over my heart and shattered it into pieces,
even now, I can't seem to glue them back together.
I sat,
the lights off,
allowed the black empty nothing to seep into my chest,
allowed the chaos to have the reins over my pain,
allowed the memories of her and I to float away to a place where
I can no longer grasp.
I couldn't tread any longer so I closed my eyes,
salty tears slid down my cheeks and hit the ground with a loud
thumping noise that made me feel less – alone.
My body ached for her hands to wrap me up just more time,
I started to beg, to plead, to appeal,
to offer my soul,
but I knew it was too late,
so instead I whispered good-bye and pushed the end button,
and sat – and sat – and sat.
I tried to breath as my lungs collapsed,
I tried to scream as my voice faded out,
I tried to recall her face – I didn't have to recall her face,
it's all that I can see.

Sold My Soul

I sold my soul to the devil,
gave her access to all my delicate parts that lay beneath my skin,
she devoured each piece,
slowly and with a desire to destroy all that I am,
all that I was,
all that I hoped to be.
My empty carcass remains,
left buried under the earth to rot.
Still,
my soul has this quiet urgency that pulls me to her,
despite the echo in my soul that screams for me to run.
I find masks hidden throughout her closet
(one for each occasion)
but I look the other way,
ignoring what I see,
casting the thoughts into a dark void,
love is blind.

Go Away

My heart beating so fast and hard that my eardrums begin to thump,
I swat away the anxiety that rises,
as if I'm swatting away a pesky fly that is trying to land on my food,
but when I look down the food is rotting before my eyes,
the paper plate turns into dust.
A bitter taste creeps in my throat and burns my mouth like a sour candy that's gone horribly bad.
My eyes search the room to see if anyone notices the sweat that's pouring from my clammy hands, or the panic look that I swear is plastered across my face,
but it goes unnoticed.
I wonder since I'm invisible would it be possible to grab a paper bag and start breathing into it because I feel that it might be my last chance for survival.
This black sky closes in on me as words flash through my mind a mile a minute,
I'm grasping at straws that don't even exist,
for the monster has already taken its place on the rightful throne of torture,
perching high that I only see the crown of thorns at the beginning of eyes that form red flames.
I wish to be swallowed by the darkness,
to remain invisible because maybe that will make the anxiety dissipate.
In this moment
(this – never the fucking right time moment)
I would like for my demons of worry to go away.

Danced with the Devil

I danced with the devil in the moonlight just before the dawn broke over the starry skies.
She wrapped her claws into my skin,
devoured all my common sense for fleeting.
I gave away pieces of myself like tokens to a party because deep down in my soul I knew she wanted to play games.
She pulled me into her and wrapped me up when she needed comfort for herself,
pushing me away with the brutal force of hatred when I asked for the same in return.
She didn't actually want me,
just the comfort that my soul brought her when she was alone.
So, we danced,
I followed her lead, her seduction took me to unknown dark places that I feared when I closed my eyes- her mayhem kept me spinning in circles,
getting me lost in the empty room.
When the daylight peaked over the horizon I let go of her hands,
broke from her lies,
I stopped dancing with the devil.

Me Against the World

I'm covered in scars that no one can see,
hidden beneath the skin of my fragile body the aches lie.
I dwell in dark places,
wondering if I'll always live there.
A quiet storm surges inside my soul,
causing a rage that forces sadness to seep from my pores.
A jealously that binds my heart,
but breaks it at the same time,
my heart collapses in on itself,
a mechanism to avoid becoming target practice for other's games.
I remind myself of the safety in solitude,
for I don't think I can break my own heart,
but one day I hope to find a home that's safe,
for now it's me against the world.

www.ingramcontent.com/pod-product-compliance
Ingram Content Group UK Ltd.
Pitfield, Milton Keynes, MK11 3LW, UK
UKHW041903190726
13854UKWH00003B/1055

9 780359 112470